YESTERDAY'S TOYS
WITH
TODAY'S PRICES

FRED AND MARILYN FINTEL

On the Cover: Desiree Fintel rides a Ben Hur Chariot Pedal Car made of heavy gauge steel with a wooden seat. It features a spare tire mounted on the back. Gear-driven, the car works on a rowing principle and can be dangerous to ride because once it is moving, the pulling mechanism and handles continue to move back and forth on their own momentum. It was manufactured in the 1920s and is 5 feet long. $125-185. Photographed at the Swenson home by Carl Bakule.

Cover Design: Ann Eastburn
Other Color Photography: Larry Hoffman
Black-and-White Photography: Craig Stellmacher and Harmon Photography Studio

Library of Congress Catalog
Card Number 84-052273

ISBN 0-87069-438-3
10 9 8 7 6 5 4 3 2 1

Published by

Wallace-Homestead Book Company
580 Waters Edge
Lombard, Illinois 60148

One of the
ABC PUBLISHING abc
Companies

Contents

1 Expert Advice on Toy Collecting

If you are seriously thinking about starting a toy collection, now is the time to begin. Prices are not getting any lower, but there are still many possibilities and types of toys to collect.

Before you start collecting, analyze the types of toys you like. Do you like action toys? Lithographed tin toys? Cast iron toys? Farm toys? Circus toys? Battery toys? Once you have decided what type or types of toys you prefer, then consider your financial means. After settling these two matters, research the toys that you are interested in collecting. Good collectors' books can be found at either the library or bookstore. From reading you should be able to determine what type of toys are within your budget. Study your research material as much as possible to learn all you can about the toys you want to collect and where they are being sold. The most likely places are antique shops, flea markets, antique shows, auctions, and garage sales. Watch the ads in local newspapers and collectors' magazines for news of where and when toys are to be found for sale. Once you have started collecting, stay current with trends and prices by reading books and trade journals on antique toys.

When purchasing toys, strive for quality rather than quantity. Someday you may want to resell the toys. You may not realize this as a beginning collector, but in time and, as your knowledge grows and your taste becomes more expensive, you may want to resell those original purchases to upgrade your collection. So right from the start, search for quality. Whether you're buying for your own satisfaction or for future resale, you'll never regret buying the best.

Another important point is if you are fortunate enough to find a toy in the original box, *never* throw away the box. Toys are very hard to find "Mint in the Original Box." This adds value to the toy. Make sure the box matches the toy to warrant the extra money, and that the toy is indeed mint. Some toys may match the box, but were played with and later returned to the box. In these cases, allow for some use in the price.

From a Woman's Point of View

There are as many women as men who collect antique toys. They may be attracted to toys for as many reasons as there are collectors. The initial exposure might come from a husband or a friend, but it doesn't take long for them to discover that toys are fascinating. Some women find the color, shape, and beauty of the toys very appealing. Others are intrigued with the investment aspect of toys.

The vibrant color and texture of fine quality toys can be a pure visual experience. Their decorative usefulness is as unlimited as the collector's imagination, and the toys make great accents throughout the home or office. Color is important, and the lithographed tin toys, with their design and detail, are truly works of art. The weight and feel of the cast iron toys and the clean lines of the old cars are irresistible to many collectors. But for pure fun, watching the action of windup toys really delights the child in all of us.

A woman should feel completely at ease decorating her office or home with antique toys. These treasures from the past will enhance any room and never cease to arouse favorable comments from visitors and guests.

For my part, I enjoy looking at and learning all about antique toys. I wouldn't buy a toy I didn't like, but I also believe toys are good investments.

—Marilyn Fintel

Buying at Auctions

It is very easy to be overwhelmed by the number of toys you will see at a toy auction. Arrive at least an hour before the bidding begins and use this time to find the toys of interest to you. Check them carefully for condition and missing pieces. Make sure that windup and battery-operated toys actually work. As you spot special toys, write down the lot numbers, condition, and the price you are willing to pay for them. Once the auction begins, do not exceed this price. If and when you make a successful bid, write down the final price you have bid for the toy.

You should also remember that some auction houses have a 5 to 10 percent buyer's fee. Keep this in mind when bidding, because this figure will be added to your final bid.

Bidding by Mail Order Auction

This is a risky business that can sometimes be useful if you understand the rules and bid accordingly. The rules were set up to protect the companies. Keep in mind that:

1 Items are sold "as is."
2 All sales are final.
3 The auction company has the right to refuse your bid.
4 The toys are not guaranteed to work.
5 The toys are not guaranteed to be originals.

Would you do business with a company having a policy like this? Antique trade magazines will list mail order toy auctions by auction house name, address, and auction date. The procedure is to write to the auction house for a catalog that could cost from $5 to $12. All of the catalogs will give the rules for buying that you should read thoroughly. The toys will be numbered and photographed with some description and condition information and, sometimes, an estimated value. The catalog will also include a bidding sheet on which you can write the catalog number, description, and your bid — remembering never to overbid a toy. Always photostat a copy of this sheet for your records as proof of your bid. Don't forget: a picture can hide a lot of scratches, dents, and missing pieces. Assume that the condition of the toy is poor when you place your bid.

After the auction the company will send you a list of all toys sold and their prices. This sold list is an excellent referral to use in determining prices and following trends in the antique toy market.

If you are a successful bidder, the company will send you a bill for the toy, or toys, and the cost of packing and shipping. Verify this statement with your copy of the bid and mail a check for the amount. They will ship the toy to you as soon as your check clears.

Grading and Pricing Toys

For our personal use we have established five classifications of toys that you may find helpful to use.

1 Mint in the Original Box.
2 Mint Condition – No Box.
3 Excellent to Very Fine.
4 Good Condition.
5 Junk or Very Poor Condition.

"Mint in the Original Box" means that the toy has never been played with and is in the original box with the original papers and wrapping still around the toy. Most importantly, the toy works. It is very rare to find a toy in Original Box condition. However, should you be so lucky, it can be worth about 25 percent more than the same toy in Mint Condition.

"Mint Condition" means that the toy has very little or no wear, no dents, and no peeling paint or missing parts. It works.

"Excellent to Very Fine" means that the toy shows some wear and tear, has been played with, but with care. All of the parts are original. It works.

"Good Condition" means that it works. There might be some rust, some wear, and some damage to the toy such as small dents, or the figures in or around the toy are bent or damaged.

"Junk or Very Poor Condition" toys do not work. However, just because a toy is rusty or broken or missing figures does not mean that it is a complete loss. The working parts can be useful at a later date as a spare parts source.

The prices you see in this book are based on a five-year study of toy auctions and antique shows. Prices can vary from area to area and are dependent upon working condition and rarity. The toys pictured all work and are generally in excellent condition. This should provide you with a general range to follow when purchasing toys for your own collection.

Dating Toys

Accurate dating, that is the exact date a toy was manufactured, is almost impossible to determine. Most toys were originally dated on the boxes, which have long since disappeared. Some toys carried paper labels that also have been lost. In some cases, the toy itself was dated, but this mark has worn off with age or use.

We get our age clues from the manufacturer. Lehmann toys were made from 1900 to 1920. Marx toys were manufactured in the 1950s along with Chein toys. Most Japanese toys were marked and date from 1940 to 1965.

A beginning collector should start by learning the manufacturers' names and years of business. This furnishes a rough time estimate. Cast iron toys, however, are a little more of a challenge. The best one can do is to estimate the date by the vehicle portrayed. You will soon learn to recognize reproductions as usually being heavier and more crudely made than the originals. Also, look at the axles. Approximately 90 percent of the reproduced axles are made of folded heavy tin, and very often you can see a seam. This is either a reproduction or an old toy with new wheels. If it doesn't look right, don't buy it.

Check the seams on a tin toy. If they overlap, the construction tells you that it was made in the 1930s. If the seams are closer together and folded, it indicates that the toy is newer and probably Japanese in origin.

You will find a Japanese symbol mark on 85 percent of the battery toys. If the toy is all plastic, it probably was made between 1960 and 1979. Toys manufactured after those years are usually marked "Made in Taiwan (or Hong Kong, or China)." Toys made in China are now available at better import stores.

Repairing Toys and Finding Parts

Repairing toys is not too difficult, and most collectors soon discover that it is not only fun, but an inexpensive way to upgrade the quality of their collection. Here are a few hints to get you started.

Beginning with the most obvious problem, keep a can of DW 40 on hand to remove rust and to repair windup toy motors. Most of the time this will loosen the rust completely, and I usually follow this treatment with a dab of 3-In-1® oil for the motor. If I'm lucky, the toy works.

If this treatment fails, check the spring mechanism to see if it is catching inside the toy or if it is broken. If so, disassemble the toy and replace the windup mechanism. (Junk toys are smart buys for spare parts.) A jeweler's screwdriver or miniature pliers is handy for this job. The most important thing to remember when taking a toy apart is to lay the parts down in sequence as they are removed so that you will have them in correct order when you put the toy back together.

Never repaint a cast iron, tin, or windup toy. Most collectors prefer their toys in original condition and will not pay good money for a repainted one.

To repair a battery-operated toy, spray DW-40 inside the working mechanism of the toy and insert new batteries. If the toy still fails to work, check the positive and negative connections. Then check the wire running from the battery housing to the toy. If this looks good and tight and the toy still doesn't operate, disassemble the toy in sequence and look for loose wires. If you still can't solve the problem, it could be the switch. However, 75 percent of the time, dead batteries, bad battery connections, or loose wiring, are usually the culprits.

If you have a toy with missing or badly damaged parts, don't worry. There are several companies in business today that manufacture headlights, sidelights, hood ornaments, bumpers, fenders, and wheels for cast iron and tin Buddy L cars and trucks. It is almost impossible to detect these replacements.

Several companies manufacture tin arms, legs, and general parts for windup toys. Personally, I do not think that it hurts the value of these toys too much to make use of these replacement parts.

There is only one company I know of that makes windup motors for toys. However, their motors do not fit the toy 85 percent of the time. I usually have more success finding good replacement motors for toys worth repairing in junk toys. Examine the junk toys at the shows and auctions for spare parts and motors. If your budget will allow their purchase, you'll find that repairing or replacing missing parts of otherwise good toys will add another dimension to your hobby and increase the value of your collection.

If you are looking for windup keys for your toys, find the names of manufacturers of replacement parts in the antique trade publications and contact them. Keys are obtainable for 90 percent of the toys found on today's market.

Guide to Toy Manufacturers

Arcade Manufacturing Company, Freeport, Illinois. The Arcade Manufacturing Company originated in 1885. The original company manufactured household items. It was not until the early 1900s that Arcade began to make cast iron toys and cast iron doll furniture. By 1920 they were well established as a maker of real and lifelike toys. During this time Arcade introduced the Yellow Taxi Cab toy that was an important factor in the success of the company. From the 1920s until the 1930s the Arcade Company was very busy making miniature cars and farm equipment. When the Great Depression came, so did hard times for this company whose toys were too expensive for the general public. When Arcade saw this happening they diversified to make souvenirs for the Chicago Century of Progress. During World War II they made military materials. After the war they went back to making toys and other non-military products, but unfortunately the market of that time was for cheaper toys such as those made of tin. The more expensive cast iron toy was not appreciated and bought. In the late 1940s the Arcade Co. went out of business.

All Arcade Toys were marked three-dimensionally with the Arcade name and/or Freeport, Ill., on the inside of the toys. They also had some paper labels with the Arcade name attached to the doors of vehicles. The paper label toys are very hard to find. This label will increase the value by 10 to 20 percent because it indicates a toy in better condition.

Chein Company, New Jersey. The Chein Company was in business from the 1930s to the 1950s. Most of the Chein Toys were sold in dimestores, because they were very reasonably priced toys. Their first toys made were their Ferris wheels and merry-go-rounds, which were large mechanical toys. These Ferris wheels and merry-go-rounds are very popular among collectors today. They also made several versions of character toys such as the popular Popeye and Brutus. Among their other toys are unique windups such as the turtle and alligator with native. All the toys made by Chein are clearly marked. I have seen no major increase in the value of these toys in the last few years. The carnival rides may continue to increase in value.

Buddy "L", Moline, Illinois. In the early 1920s Fred Lundahl who owned the Moline Pressed Steel Company made a few special toys for his son Buddy. When Buddy's friends wanted these same toys, Fred Lundahl found himself in the toy business. So from manufacturing full-scale auto and truck parts he began making parts on a much smaller scale. Still as far as toy cars and trucks go the 21 to 24 inch size of most of these Buddy "L" toys is larger than most toys. They are made of a very sturdy steel.

The Buddy "L" Toy Co. is still in business today making high quality toys at a reasonable price. These Buddy "L" toys are marked by a paper label on the side of the toy. Without the label some of the clues to indicate a Buddy "L" toy are their large size and the iron wheels. They are made of heavy gauge steel.

Hubley Manufacturing Co., Lancaster, Pennsylvania. In 1984 John Hubley started the Hubley Manufacturing Company. Up until World War this company manufactured cast iron toys of a high quality that were very attractive. During the war the Hubley Manufacturing Company was engaged almost entirely in making war-related materiel. After the war, when they resumed toy manufacturing, the toys were no longer made of cast iron but constructed of die cast metal and plastic. It is the older cast iron toys made before the war that are now very collectible. Pre-war toys were marked with the name stamped inside the toy. After the war Hubley toys were given a three-dimensional mark on the outside.

Kenton Hardware Manufacturing Co., Kenton, Ohio. In 1894 the Kenton Hardware Manufacturing Company began making toys. Kenton made single-unit vehicles, but they are most famous for horse-drawn toys produced up until 1954. Most of the Kenton toys are unmarked. Be very careful of the reproductions that are made overseas. When a marking is found, it should be stamped U.S.A. and numbered on the connecting rods of the vehicles. The numbers were used to match up the assembly of pieces. These toys are rare to find in the original box with the original wax wrapping paper.

Ernst Paul Lehmann Company, Brandenburg, Germany. The Lehmann Company first went into business in 1881. They made toys up until 1928. These toys were popular in Germany and other European countries. Some American tourists who visited Germany brought these toys back with them. Also some large department stores imported the Lehmann Toys. They were not too popular as they were expensive and very fragile. Therefore, not many of these toys have survived. They were not desirable to play with but rather were nice as a shelf piece. Today the price of these hard to find toys can average from two hundred to twelve hundred dollars a toy. They are very hard to find in mint condition. All Lehmann toys are marked with the initials E.P.L. and "Lehmann." When purchasing a Lehmann Toy be sure to look over the toy carefully as about 75 percent of these toys have replacement pieces. In my years of collecting I have found very few all-original Lehmanns.

Lindstrom Company, U.S.A. From the 1930s to the 1950s the Lindstrom Company manufactured such toys as "Sweeping Mammy" and "Dancing Lassie," which are dancing shako toys. Only a few of the Lindstrom Toys have a great value, except the Parcel Post truck, of which they made only a few. They also made a dancing couple that featured a white man and woman. This toy is very rare. I have seen only one in good shape. Most Lindstrom toys are black character toys. All Lindstrom Toys are marked on the back, "Lindstrom U.S.A."

Louis L. Marx Toy Company, New York. The Louis Marx Toy Company came into existence in about 1921 when Louis Marx began making toys with his brother as an independent company. Before this Louis Marx worked for the Strauss Company. By the 1950s the Louis Marx Company was the largest maker of toys of that time. Not just here in the United States but also abroad. Louis Marx's aim in the toy market of his day was to give quality at the cheapest price possible. Tin windups were the most popular of his models. In addition to the tin windups, the Marx Company made play sets with tin buildings, such as dollhouses, gas stations, army and farm sets. These play sets are not as collectible as the other Marx toys. In the future they may become more desirable. Marx also made high quality trains and train accessories. All Marx toys were marked. The early toys were marked "Louis Marx." When the company reorganized in the 1930s they were then marked "Marx." Louis Marx died at the age of eighty-five in 1982. The company went out of business in the 1980s.

Ohio Art, Bryan, Ohio. The Ohio Art Company was founded in 1908. During the First World War they began to produce toys. Their lithographed metal tea sets were produced during the early years of business. From 1934 to 1958 this toy company was at its best. They are the makers of the most famous tops, drums, and sand pails. In the 1950s plastic toys were introduced. All their toys are clearly marked.

2 Aeronautical Toys

General

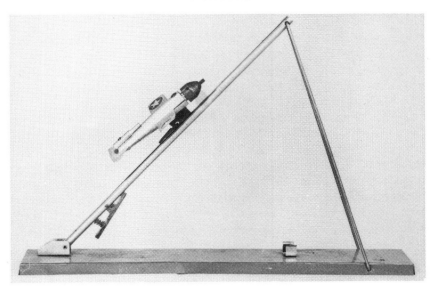

Cata-Bo Jet Bomb, made by Sallow Mfg. Co., C. 1940, pull-action, 17″ long, 11″ high, **$38-52.** Not for a child. Dangerous. The rocket pulls back and locks. Has a trigger action that fires rocket hard and fast.

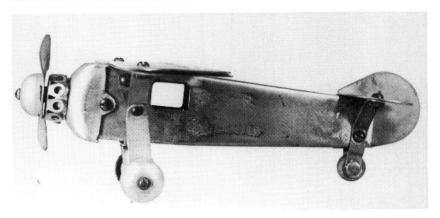

Spirit of St. Louis, made by Metalcraft, C. 1940, in kit form, 8½″ long, wingspan 11½″, **$50-85.** These were sold in kits to be assembled at home.

Baby Blimp (Zeppelin), maker unknown, C. 1930, pull toy, 8" long, **$50-75.** A nice addition to a Zeppelin collection.

Buck Rogers Battlecruiser, by Tootsie Toy, C. 1930, string operation, 4½" long, **$60-110.** They also made Buck Rogers Flash Attack Ship valued at $55-100 and Venus Duo-Destroyer valued at $55-100. These string rockets all in pot metal.

Airplane, unmarked, C. 1930, push, 21½" long, 22½" wide, 6" high, **$45-65.** Made of folded metal. Body and wing are bolted together. When pulled, the propeller goes around and makes a motor noise.

Rocket Car, unmarked, made from very heavy folded metal. C. 1940, push, 6" long, 2½" high, **$25-32.** Undercarriage is green, top is red, tail is purple, and the wheels are black. Very colorful.

U.S.N. Los Angeles, made by Tootsie Toy, C. 1930, string, 4½″ long, **$50-75.** Metal dirigibles were sold in Buck Rogers' sets in 1937. All have about the same value.

Left to right: Cast iron Zep, made by Dent, C. 1930, pull, 5″ long, **$25-50.** This Zeppelin is hard to find with the original wheels. Highly collectible. Collectors have been known to pay dearly for this toy with or without the wheels. Pony Blimp, unmarked, C. 1930, pull, 5½″ long, **$30-60.** Toy has three wheels. Has a tendency to fall over when being pulled.

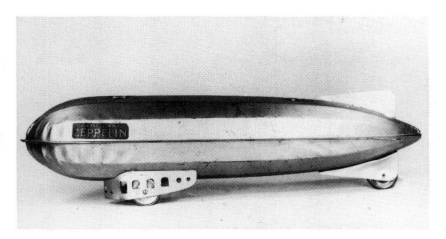

Little Giant Zeppelin, unmarked, 1939, pull, 26″ long, 7½″ high, **$50-80.** Made from tin painted silver. Underneath the fuselage is a metal spring. When the toy is pulled, it makes a motor noise. Hard to find with all the original decals.

Windup

Graf Zeppelin with Eagle mark on bottom. Made by Strauss, C. 1930s, windup, 17″ long, **$300-500.** Tail is marked "GZ2017;" made of very thin aluminum.

Los Angeles Zeppelin made by Strauss, C. 1930s, windup, 9½" long, **$300-400.** Zeppelins are very collectible at the present time and very difficult to find in the original box and with the propellers intact.

Zeppelin, unmarked, C. 1930, windup, 9¼" long, **$45-65.** Folded tin. Toy has wooden back wheel and two tin front wheels. Very similar to other Zeppelins, but has no propeller. Marked Zeppelins are the high quality toys.

Unmarked Zeppelin, C. 1930s, windup, 10½" long, **$45-75.** Toy is made of folded tin and unusual because it has a back tail wind with the propeller in front.

Zeppelin, unmarked, C. 1930s, windup, 9½" long, **$45-65.** Made of folded metal with an undercarriage wind and the propeller in the back.

3 Banks

Mechanical

Southern Comfort, unmarked, C. 1960, lever action, 6″ high, 8″ long, **$22-30.** Also given as bank premiums. Made of cast metal and aluminum and highly painted.

Feeding ducks, made in Japan, C. 1960s coin operated, 4" high, 4" wide, **$12-15.**
Hard plastic. Ducks peck up and down when coin activates the mechanism.

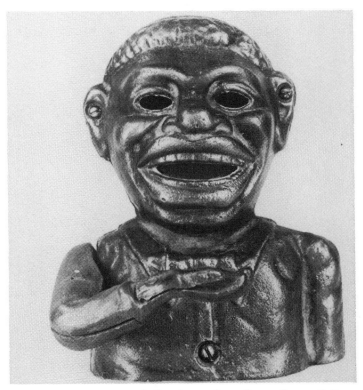

Mechanical banks are rarely found at antique shows, flea markets, or antique shops. Always purchase a mechanical bank from a reputable dealer. If you want to research these banks, there are books showing patterns of bank bottoms. However, knowing the bottom pattern does not guarantee an original bank, as an old bottom can be put on a new bank.

The Jolly Nigger is a good example. It is a reproduction worth about **$15.** An original is worth about **$250.** As you can see, it is clearly marked.

Mercury rocket mechanical bank made by Duro, C. 1950-1960, lever action, 2½" high, 8" long, **$22-30.** Banks gave away thousands of these banks as premiums for opening savings accounts. Also found in different forms (cars, boats, airplanes), and made in cast metal and aluminum.

Still

Left to right: U.S. Tank Bank, unknown, C. 1930, cast iron, 2" high, 4" long, **$55-75.** There are three larger tank banks on the market that have a higher value. Sitting and Smiling Pig, unknown, C. 1930, cast iron, 3" high, 4" long, **$55-70.** Various sizes of the pig bank are available and are priced accordingly.

Sidewheel bank, unmarked, C. 1930, cast iron, 7½" long, 2½" high, **$105-165.** Approximately seven different sizes of boat banks were made. Most were smaller than this example. There is one larger than this model. All have roughly the same value. This is a very nice toy and bank.

Left to right: Time to Save bank, made by Kingsbury Mfg. Co., C. 1940, 7" high, **$40-60**. This bank is made from metal and takes nickels, dimes, quarters (no pennies). When it reaches a total of $9.95-10.00, automatic release on the bottom opens the trapdoor. The same company made toy trucks and cars. These banks are not popular accessory pieces with collectors or bank collectors. The Cash Register bank is made from heavy tin and will only take dimes. Unmarked, C. 1940, 4½" long, 4" high, **$35-50**. Register totals the amount deposited up to a maximum of $9.90. There is no release to retrieve the money. There were gold stencil markings across the top that have worn off.

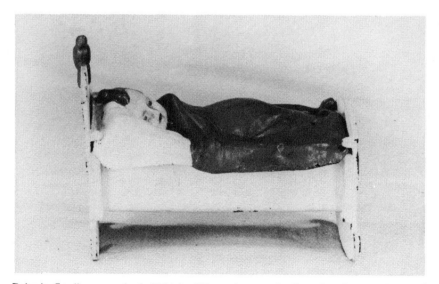

Baby in Cradle, unmarked, 3" high, 4" long, is reproduction of earlier cast iron and steel model. Reproduction has coin slot on side, is heavier. **$10-20**. If original with coin slot on top, value would be **$95-165**.

4 Battery-Operated Toys

Animals

Hy-Que, made by Alps of Japan, 1948, 14″ high, **$100-125.** One of the rarest battery-operated toys we have found. When you shake its hand, the hand moves to indicate "Speak No Evil, Hear No Evil, See No Evil."

Fishing Bear, made by Alps of Japan, C. 1960, 12″ high, **$45-60.** Not to be confused with the Fishing Kitty which was made in the 1950s and is worth $70-100.

Mama Bear and Hungry Baby Bear, made by the Y Co., C. 1950, 9½" high, **$70-90** (MIB). This is a five-action toy. Rarely found with the liquid in the bottle.

Dentist Bear, made in Japan, 1959, 11" high, **$65-75.** Rare to find this toy with liquid that sprays from the mouth when activated.

Barber Bear, made by T. M. Co., 1959, 12″ high, **$70-85.** Very desirable due to the amount of action.

The Burger Chef shakes salt on the hamburger, his ears go straight up when he flips the hamburger, and he never misses the catch. Made by the Y Co., C. 1950, 9½" high, **$60-90.**

Be careful buying the Musical Chimp. It is being reproduced today in Taiwan. This one was made by the Alps Co., C. 1960, 10½" high, **$25-35.** Note the low price for an old toy.

Frankie, the Roller Skating Monkey, made in Japan, C. 1950, 11½" high, **$60-75.** Monkey skates back and forth and moves his hands.

Piggy Cook is a five-action toy. He moves his lithographed eggs from side to side, shakes pepper on them, flips them, and in conclusion, his chef hat puffs up. Made by Y. of Japan, C. 1950s, battery, 10½" high, 4" long, **$40-75.**

Pianist, made in Japan, C. 1950s, 8¼" high, **$100-125.** This dog plays
the piano and moves his head. Similar to the Musical Bulldog made in the
1950s by Sam Co. The Bulldog is the rarer of the two.

Barking Dog, made in Taiwan, C. 1970, 12″ long, **$15-20.** This toy is leash operated. Pull the leash once and he walks; pull twice and the dog stops, barks, and wags his tail.

Characters

Balloon Vendor is a four-action toy made by the Y. Co. of Japan, C. 1960, 12″ high, **$45-65.** Worth $3-5 more in the original box.

Charlie Weaver, made by T-N Co., 1962, 12″ high, **$45-65.** Six-action toy. Not to be confused with bartender toy that has three bar stools painted on the front and bartender wearing a dinner jacket. Charlie Weaver is worth twice as much money.

Old Man Drinking, made in Japan, C. 1950, battery, 12″ high, **$33-48.**
Not a very popular toy in our opinion.

A lot of nice action in this Twist Dancer toy. Made by Haji Co., 1955, 12″ high, **$65-90.**

Cragstan Crap Shooter, made by the Y Co., C. 1950, 9½" high, **$60-85.**
Four-action toy. Hard to find with the original dice.

In good condition Indian Joe will beat drum and make mouth noises. Made by Alps Co., C. 1960, 12" high, **$45-65.**

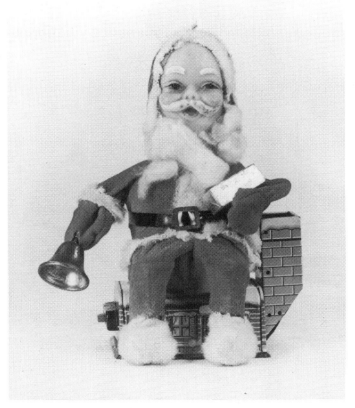

Santa Claus Bell Ringer, made by Alps of Japan, C. 1950, 10½" high, **$55-70.** One action toy, not too popular.

Circus Clown on Tricycle, made in Taiwan, C. 1970, 11″ high, **$10-20.**
Unusual because the batteries go in the bottom of the clown. You must
remove the clown from the tricycle to replace batteries. In action the
clown pedals the tricycle.

Walking Santa Claus, made in Taiwan, C. 1980, 12″ high, **$12-15.**
Reproduction of 1960s 10″ Santa made by T.M. Co. Both are three-
action toys.

In the 1950s Y of Japan made many Western character toys. They are approximately same value. Gunfighter walks and shoots, 11″ high, **$60-75.**

Robots

Gigantor Robot was made by Mego of Hong Kong, C. 1960, 15½" high, **$40-55.** Gigantor walks, stops, opens his chest, turns twice and fires light beams, then stops and walks on.

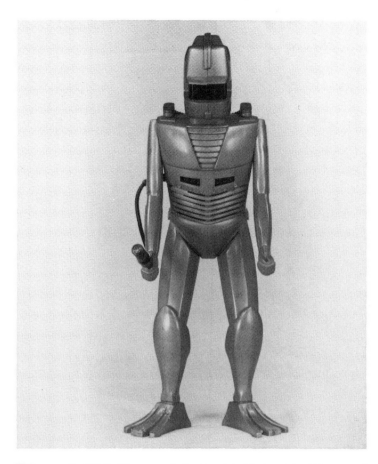

This unmarked Robot has a toy helmet and tool in hand that light up and chest lights that blink right and left. C. 1970, 13" high, **$20-30.**

Collecting robots has become very popular in the past three to five years. Prices on robots from the 1950s and 1960s are considerably higher than those from the 1970s. Most of them have lights, lots of action and color, and are hard to find. Piston Robot, made by S.J.M. of Taiwan, C. 1970, 10½", is worth **$25-40.**

Vehicles

Pioneer Spirit, made in Japan, C. 1955, 12″ long, **$45-65.** Cute action toy.

Skylark Funicular, made by T-N Co., C. 1950, 12″ long, **$55-75.** This toy has a string that threads through the wheels and sticks on a wall. As the toy moves and bumps the wall, the flags go up and down.

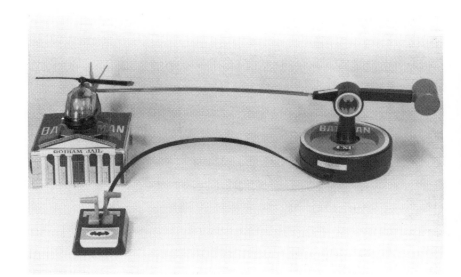

Look for Batman helicopters at flea market sales. Made in Japan, C. 1970, assembles, **$20-35.** Be sure to get all of the parts.

Mystery Car, made by T. N. of Japan, C. 1950, 9″ long, **$60-75.** Called a Mystery Car because the head pops off when the car stops.

Watch for this collectible — we think it will go up in value. Volkswagen, made by Bendai Co., C. 1960, 9" long, **$15-25.**

Dune Buggy, made in Japan and imported by Bandal, C. 1960, 8" long, 4" high, **$22-30.** Battery housing is see-through plastic, and the car is steel and plastic.

Fire Department Car, made in Japan, C. 1950, 9½" long, **$35-55.** Has forward and reverse drive button on the powerpack. When the car is moving, the top lights. Rare to find this plastic toy as most of them melted in the sun or were broken. If found in the original box, add $10 to value.

5 Cast Iron Toys

Boats

Sidewheeler boat is very clearly marked Priscilla on the outside. Made by Dent or Wilkens, C. 1920 or older, cast iron, 10½" long, **$225-350.**

This paddlewheel boat makes a nice paperweight. It was made C. 1940, 1½" high by 4½" long. **$12-25.**

Horse-drawn Vehicles

Animal Cage of the Overland Circus, made by Kenton, C. 1940, 14" long, **$240-400.** Must have the bear, driver, and two riders to warrant full value. Same toy was made in the 1950s, 13" long, and we have no idea as to why it is worth only $60. All boxes are marked Kenton Hardware Co.

Overland Circus Bandwagon, made by Kenton, C. 1940, 15" long, **$200-300.** For full value this must have all six band players, the driver, and two horse riders. The figures are being reproduced today, so be careful.

There are many reproductions of these cast iron toys on the market. Pay only a reasonable amount of money for these toys unless you are sure the toy is authentic and can verify that it is an original model. *Left to Right:* Fire Truck with ladder, unmarked, C. 1940, cast iron, 4″ long, 2″ high, **$45-65.** Horse-drawn Ladder Truck, unknown, C. 1940, 5″ long, 2½″ high, **$55-90.**

Horse-drawn Surrey, made by Stanley, C. 1950, 11½″ long, **$35-65.** Very common and not a recommended investment.

Unmarked Horse-drawn Hook and Ladder, C. early 1900, 30½" long, 8½" high, **$400-625.** The number 126 is marked on side of ladder wagon. It is nickel-plated, has wooden ladders, and horses prance up and down when the toy is moved.

Horse-drawn Cart, unmarked, C. 1930, 7" long, 3" high, **$75-95.** Toy is made of cast iron and tin and is very fragile. We're surprised it has lasted this long.

Horse-drawn Cart, unmarked, 1912, iron and tin, 7″ long, 3″ high, **$45-75.** From 1900-1920 there were many horse-drawn toys made with iron horses and wheels. The carts were always tin. They have different values.

Horse-drawn Chariot, unmarked, C. 1930, 7″ long, **$50-65.** Most of these toys are now minus the rider.

Spark Plugs, unmarked, C. 1940, pull, 4½″ long, 3½″ high, **$22-36.** This is made out of pot metal. Most of these toys had small, hard rubber wheels. We have also seen wooden wheels. We think they were made both ways.

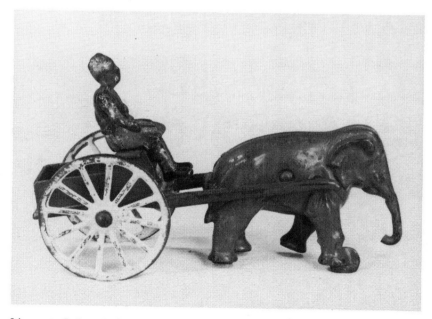

It's rare to find an elephant cart with an Indian driver. This one was made in the 1930s, 8″ long, 5″ high, **$225-325.**

Motorized Vehicles

Buddy L Army Truck, C. 1940, push toy; 21″ long, **$45-65.** All Buddy L Army trucks came with a cloth top marked U. S. Army. Truck and cloth were Army green.

Mack Stake Truck, made by Champion, C. 1930, 7½″ long, **$180-300.** Original wheels were rubber; 75 percent of these trucks have new wheels. We don't think that the new wheels affect the value much.

Fire Pumper, unmarked, 1935, 8″ long, **$55-95.** Original toy had cast iron wheels. This one has rubber reproduction wheels.

This toy is being reproduced. Buy it carefully. Firepumper, unmarked, C. 1930, 6¼″ long, 3½″ high, **$60-100.**

Steam Shovel Digger Truck, made by Hubley, C. 1949-1955, push toy, 9" long, 3½" high, **$35-55.** Has nickel-plated front bumper, scoop, and scoop arm. It should appreciate in value.

Mack Gas Truck, unmarked, C. 1920, 4½" long, 2½" high, **$75-95.** Could be a Kenton or Hubley. It has nickel-plated spoke wheels. Very unique for a small piece.

Bus, unmarked, C. 1930, 1½" high, 4½" long, **$50-75.** This toy looks like the five window Arcade bus, but is ½" shorter. The inside is marked with a number but no other identification.

Unmarked Dump Truck, C. 1930, push toy, 16" long, 7" high, **$75-125.** This is a very heavy and durable steel toy.

Many cast iron motorcycles were made in the 1930s. Most of the sidecars are missing passengers or have reproduced passengers. This model was made by Hubley, is 2½" high, 4" long, **$45-60.**

This unmarked Racer is similar to the Kenton boat-tail cutdown speedster made in 1910. The Kenton model is 7" long and has greater value. This C. 1920 model is 6½" long, **$40-70.**

Dump Truck, made by Arcade, C. 1920, 10½" long, **$200-350.** Arcade made about ten different models of trucks. Also called International Harvester or Red Baby trucks.

Unknown cars and truck, C. 1930, 3¼" long, 1½" high, **$55-75 each.** All three of these vehicles have two pieces and are very unusual. A wire runs along the bottom to hold the wheels in place. Nuts and bolts hold the pieces together.

Hubley Fire Truck with Ladder, C. 1930, 5″ long, 2″ high, **$45-65.** This toy has rubber wheels and separate iron ladders. Marked on undercarriage.

Unmarked truck, made in 1934, cast iron, 10″ long, **$95-125.** These toys were sold during the Century of Progress Show in Chicago 1933-1934. They are very hard to find mint with the original painting and lettering across the top.

Merry Makers Mouse Band by Marx, C. 1930, is a litho tin windup. Marx made two versions of this toy. The other version has a half-moon shaped shield on top of the piano that reads "Merry Makers." Both have approximately the same value and are about 10¼" long, 10¼" high, **$585-625.**

This litho tin piece has great action. Li'l Abner dances, Mammy directs, Pappy plays the drums, and Daisy Mae plays the piano. Make sure Mammy has her pipe and all other pieces are intact and original. Made by Unique Art, 1945, windup, 10" long, 8" high, **$250-395.**

Circus Cage of Overland Circus, made by Kenton, C. 1940, cast iron, 14″ long, **$240-400.** Must have bear, driver, and two horses to warrant full value. The same toy made in the 1950s is 13″ long, and we have no idea as to why it is worth only $60. All boxes are marked Kenton Hardware Co.

Be careful when purchasing the Overland Band Wagon. The figures are being reproduced, and for full value this toy must have all six band players, the driver, and two horse riders. Made by Kenton, C. 1940, cast iron, 15″ long, **$200-300.**

Zilotone by Wolverine, litho tin windup made C. 1930, 8" long, 7¼" high. When the toy is wound up, place a metal record on the top back of the toy. As it unwinds the standing man plays the recorded music. This toy usually came with six records. If the toy doesn't work, don't buy it regardless of condition. The windup mechanism is so strong it is impossible to repair. **$165-300.**

Climbing Miller by Lehmann is weight driven. To make the toy work, hook the lead flour sack on the hook found at the top side of the toy. This will cause the Climbing Miller to climb to the top. The flour sack then releases on top of his head and he comes back down. This toy is hard to find with the original lead flour sack and cardboard blades. It dates from the 1920s and is 16½" high. **$175-295.**

Left to right: Milton Berle, wearing a plastic hat, drives a very sporty car with writing on all four sides, 5½" long, 6" high, **$95-135.** The Joe Penner Wanna Buy a Duck windup toy is 8" high, **$145-245.** Joe walks, tips his hat, and his cigar moves up and down.

Left to right: G.I. Joe and the K-9 Pups litho tin made by Unique Art Co., C. 1940, 9" high, **$65-95.** An easy toy for the beginning collector to find is G.I. Joe and his Bouncing Jeep, also made by Unique Art, C. 1940, 6½" high, 6¼" long, **$65-125.**

During the years that Marx was in business they made hundreds of these bucking cars from litho tin and plastic. They range in value from $70 to $350 each at present. All Marx toys are clearly marked "Marx." *Left to right:* note the print on the litho tin Joy Rider's car and suitcase mounted on the rear. Made in 1928-1929, it is 7" long, 6" high, **$145-195.** This car is rarely found with the suitcase still attached. Charlie McCarthy is 8" long, 6" high, **$160-250.** Charlie's head makes a complete circle as the car moves back and forth.

Left to right: Drumming Indian, made by Alps Co., Japan, C. 1960, 12″ high, **$45-65.** In good condition Indian Joe will play the drum and make mouth noises. Mother Feeding Baby Bear is battery-operated, made by the Y Co., Japan, C. 1950, 9½″ high, **$70-90** (M.I.B.). This five-action toy rarely found with liquid in the bottle.

Some appealing windup toys, made in Japan, C. 1950. *Left to right:* Drumming Bear, 6″ high, **$25-35.** Circus Clown made like the Schuco toy of Charlie Chaplin in the 1920s, 8″-9½″ high, **$50-65.** Reading Bear is a two-action toy. The bear's head moves up and down as he flips pages in his book, 5″ high, **$22-36.**

Alabama Coon Jigger litho tin windup by Lehmann, C. 1914, 10″ high, **$295-425.** Two versions of this toy were made. This is the more expensive with a trip lever on the side. The other version has the trip lever on the front of the toy. Ampol, C. 1903, 5″ high, 5″ long, **$780-1,200.**

Amos 'n' Andy Fresh Air Taxi is litho tin windup. The car moves, stops, shakes, and repeats the action. Made by Marx, C. 1930, 8″ long, 5″ high, **$300-500.**

A nice assortment of cast iron toys. Beginning collectors should be careful to buy from a reputable dealer or certain they know the markings. Every day more reproduction cast iron toys are being made and introduced on the open market.

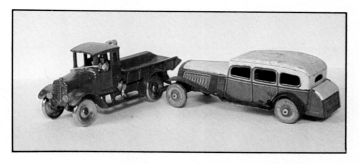

Left to right: Dump Truck, made by Arcade, C. 1920, cast iron, 10½" long, **$200-350.** English Sedan, made in England, C. 1930, windup, 11" long, 4" high, **$145-225.** This is a very unusual and unique toy that we expect to increase in value.

Left to right: Royal Van Co. windup by Marx, C. 1929-1933, is made from very thin, folded tin with nice lithography. Hard to find with original driver, 4" high, 9" long, **$60-85.** Very rare and fragile friction wheel automobile, made in Germany, litho tin penny toy, C. 1920, 4½" long, **$150-225.**

Left to right: Rolls Royce, marked A-1, made by Sakura of Japan, Mercedes, marked A-2, and Jaguar, marked A-1. This company went out of business in 1963. They also made airplane robots and several kinds of space fantasy toys. The value of these three cars is approximately **$32-45 each.** A 1963 four-door Cadillac, also by Sakura (not pictured) is the most valuable and rare.

The gray German windup car on the left was originally made as a remote control car. We have seen only one working and complete. **$95-165.** The yellow car on the right is a key windup, has a shift lever mechanism, runs forward or backward, and the steering wheel turns right or left. Produced in yellow, gray, and red, 9½″ long, 2½″ high, **$95-129.**

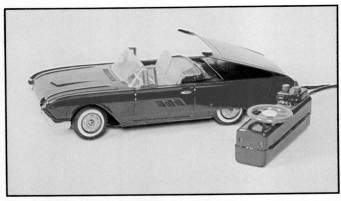

Japanese-made, battery-operated Thunderbird with retractable hardtop has a forward and reverse operation. Retractable top is very unusual. C. 1960, 11″ long, **$60-85.**

6 Disney and Other Character Toys

Banks

Disney character banks were made with tree trunks, baskets, or barrels. All were painted pot metal. Value runs from **$40-80,** depending upon condition. This cute model is Porky Pig, maker unknown, 4½" high, 6" long, C. 1950, **$40-65.**

Elmer Fudd and Basket, maker unknown, C. 1950, pot metal bank, 4½″ high, 6″ long, **$40-65.**

Beaky, maker unknown, C. 1950, pot metal bank, 4½″ high, 6″ long, **$40-65.**

74

Battery-Operated

Mickey Mouse Sand Buggy, made by Marx, C. 1960, 6½" high, **$70-90.** Very unique and unusual toy. Mickey spins the inside wheels right and left and the toy moves right and left across surface. Plastic.

Push-Pull

Donald Duck Car, by Sun Rubber, C. 1930, push, 6½" long, **$32-50.** Made of hard rubber with rubber wheels. Came in red, yellow, and orange. All colors have the same value.

Mickey's Tractor came in various colors that affect the value of the toy. This was made C. 1930, 4½", **$32-65.** Mickey's head turns.

Mickey's Air Mail, by Sun Rubber Co., C. 1930, 4½" long, **$25-50.** This toy is made from hard rubber and has rubber wheels. It is our feeling that Disney rubber character toys have peaked in price and popularity.

Windup

Pinocchio the Acrobat is a very unique Disney action toy, made by Marx in 1939. The platform rocks back and forth while Pinocchio flips back and forth. Clearly marked "Walt Disney Productions," 17" high, 11" long, **$135-250.**

If you find this toy, make sure the head of Donald Duck is original. Donald Duck Hand Car, made by Lionel Corporation, C. 1940, 9¼″ long, 7″ high, **$225-350.** Lionel is planning to reissue this toy in 1985 or 1986.

Goofy Wheelbarrow, by Marx, C. 1960, 5″ high, 5″ long, **$10-22.** Hard plastic toy moves along the surface with Goofy's legs running mechanically. Not to be confused with Goofy the Walking Gardener made by Marx in the 1930s that is bigger, made of tin, and worth $400-700.

Lithographed tin Donald Duck car, made by Marx, 1950s, 6″ high, 5½″ long, **$60-125.** Donald Duck is plastic and the car is made like the Mickey Mouse car with Mickey's mark. Donald's head is on a spring, and when the car moves, his head wiggles.

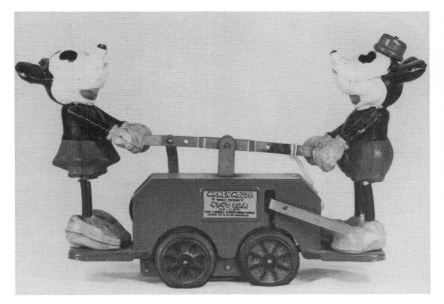

Mickey Mouse Hand Car, made by Lionel, C. 1940, 7″ long, **$300-500.** Made with a green, orange, and red base, with red the most common. Make sure Mickey's hat is original.

Left and right: Donald Duck, Goofy, and Mickey Mouse are nodders made by Marx, C. 1940, 1½-2″ high, **$15-22 each.** These toys had Marx paper labels on bottoms, and are just a few of the Disney toys made by Marx. Collectors like them because they are cute. *Center:* Cinderella and Prince Charming, made in the U.S.A. by Irwin, C. 1950, 5¼″ high, **$60-75.** Made of plastic, and, when wound, they dance across the surface.

Pluto by Marx, 1939, windup tail, 10″ long, **$65-110.** Litho tin, dated on the side, produced by Walt Disney. Winding tail causes him to move across surface. Similar to Pluto Dog "Watch Me Roll Over," made by the same company in 1939 and has equal value.

7 Farm Toys

Farm toys have become very desirable collectibles in the past ten years. We feel this popularity stems from many sources. Young people working in the city remember the days when they played with these toys or actually used the farm vehicle at home. Owners are collecting replicas of their current farm equipment, and retired farmers enjoy owning these miniature reminders of the past. For these reasons and more, farm toys are hot items today.

John Deere tractors have jumped in value from $25 to $350 per toy tractor in just five years. Accessory pieces are also in demand.

These farm vehicles are being collected in groupings or series. Collectors have been known to pay a premium to complete a series. Good construction, such as hard rubber wheels, real steering, tin rims on wheels, etc., also add value to the toy. Rural areas tend to generate higher prices than metropolitan areas.

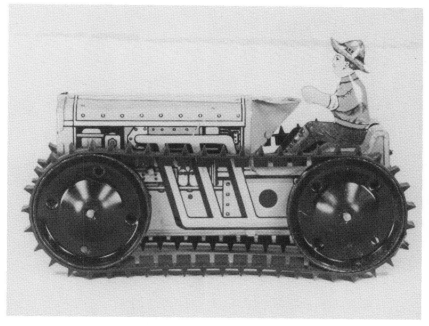

Caterpillar, made by Marx, C. 1950, litho tin windup, 8½" long, 4" high, **$40-55.** The tracks are rubber with a climbing action. These were made from the 1920s to the 1960s. Add $2-5 if in original box.

Future collectible? Road graders, steam shovels, etc., are not too popular at the time. This International bulldozer was made C. 1960, push action, pot metal, 9½″ long, 3½″ high, **$25-30.** Good buy now.

Left to right: John Deere Tractor 60 and accessories, made by Ertl, C. 1950, push, 4½″ high, 8″ long, **$75-125.** Painted metal construction. Hard rubber wheels, Tin wheel inserts. Steering action, and good detail.

Avery Tractor, marked Avery, C. 1930, cast iron, 4½″ long, 3″ high, **$100-165.** Take care to purchase an original, not a reproduction. In most cases, old tractors have new wheels.

Unusual tractor marked Super Six Junior. Made in the 1950s, 13½″ long, 5½″ high, **$45-60.** Push the seat down and the shovel lifts. Lever on side dumps the shovel. The other lever winds the mechanism.

A silver, postwar Caterpillar, made by Marx, windup, 8″ long, 4″ high, **$40-55.** This toy is all silver.

8 Fisher-Price

Rabbit Cart, pull toy, C. 1960, 9½″ high, 10″ long, **$50-75.** Recently Fisher-Price toys have taken a nice jump in value. The older toys are made of wood and have wooden wheels. We expect the toys with plastic wheels to increase in value in time. Toys showing no increase as yet, are Fisher-Price buildings, such as the schoolhouse, motels, restaurants, etc.

Left to right: Pelican pull toy, 1950-1960, 8″ high, 7″ long, **$25-35.** Wooden with plastic beak and feet. Fisher-Price toys are all numbered and this Pelican is 794. Toys made of wood with wooden wheels and paper labels are very collectible. Value depends upon the numbers on them. Prices also vary according to the amount of lithographed paper left on toy. Bossy Bell pull toy, 1950-1960, 6″ long, 5½″ high, **$20-25.** Number 656 is behind the front wheel and very hard to find.

9 Friction Toys

Siren Sparkling Fire Engine by Marx, 1927, 9¼" long, **$100-145.** Undercarriage and wheels are very clearly marked.

Space Sight-Seeing Bus, made in Japan, C. 1960, 6" long, 3¼" high, litho tin, **$18-22.** When pushed, the friction wheels make the center of the toy light red and green.

Litho tin Penny Toy, German, C. 1920, 4½″ long, **$150-225.** Made from very thin tin. Fragile and rare.

Japanese-made 1929 sedan, C. 1950, 7¼″ long, 3″ high, **$25-45.** Many of these on the market, but hard to find in the original box. We think they will go up in value in the future.

Watching trends? We pick the Future Car, made in Japan, C. 1960, 8½" long, **$12-22.**
Readily available at flea markets, antique shows, and antique shops.

Race Car No. 65, made by Mattel, 1965, 11½" long, **$12-20.** Made of lightweight metal with metallic paint, these are difficult to find in mint condition. Only the wheels are marked Mattel. We think they will go up in value. The 1940s and 1950s race cars are high priced today.

Flip-over Motorcycle, Alps of Japan, early 1950s, 5″ high, 5¼″ long, litho tin, **$30-45.**
To start the engine, you must push it and hold the side lever in at the same time. When
the lever is released, it flips over. The driver moves up and down.

Another future winner? Tricky Tricycle, by Y of Japan, C. 1950, 6″ long, 6½″ high,
$22-30. When pushed, the dog moves back and forth. Siren noise. Very colorful litho
tin.

Another winner! Jet Car, made by Ideal, C. 1960, friction and windup, 13½" long, 4½" high, **$65-95.** Car has a friction siren motor. The car platform has a crank system and the car slides and locks into it. The back of the platform is cranked and the car is released by pushing button on side. Lots of action and speed.

10 Miscellaneous Toys

Jumping Ford, made in Japan, C. 1940, spring, 1½" high, 4" long, **$5-10.** Also made in two other sizes. This is the smallest. All have about the same value.

Very fragile celluloid animals, marked "Made in U.S.A.," C. 1940-1950s, 3-5½" long, **$12-22 each.** Most were sand-filled to weigh them down.

Simplex Typewriter, C. 1950-1960, push type, 8½″ long, **$18-30.** During this period of time Marx, Chein, and other companies all made toy typewriters of this type. All have equal value.

Painted tin Thrill Ride, unmarked, C. 1940, gravity action, 16½″ high, 10½″ long, **$75-125.** Car is placed at top and released to spin in circular motion. Then wire catches the car and spins it around. Lots of these toys around, but most are minus the cars and the catch wheels don't work. Not a very popular toy.

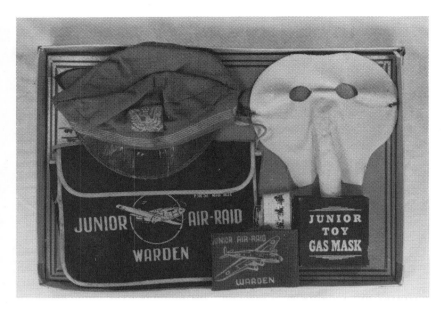

Junior Air-Raid Warden, made by Boys-D-Lite, C. 1940, 20″ long, 12″ wide, **$35-50.**
These dress-up play sets came in different styles — cowboy, policeman, soldier, and
Indian. They also made sets for girls such as nurse, waitress, secretary, and WAC.
Very hard to find.

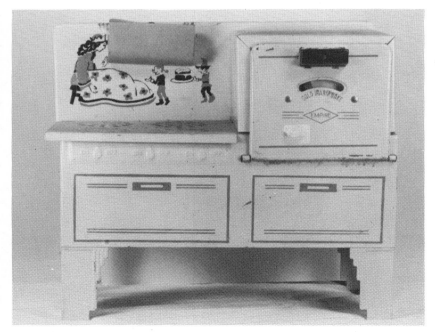

Electric Stove, made by Empire, litho tin C. 1940, electric, 11″ long, 10″ high, **$22-
36.** The Little Orphan Annie version is the most desirable child's stove. It is similar to
this one except oven is on the bottom.

B-22 Battleship, made by Keystone, C. 1940, wood, 18″ long, 4½″ high, **$25-45.** Boat must be complete with metal guns, airplane on front, and bullets that go into guns to be worth top price. Few metal toys were made during the war years.

Shooting Gallery, lithographed tin, made by Wyandotte, C. 1950, windup, 11″ high, 14″ long, **$20-35.** The target rotates and the ducks move. Wyandotte also made the "Posse Shooting Gallery," which is more desirable.

Cash Register, by Buddy L, C. 1940, mechanical, 10½" long, 9" high, **$60-95**. Made from heavy metal by the same company that made the large Buddy L toys. Front of this toy has three sliding levers with numbers that slide to ring up price. Price is printed on paper tape inside. The machine then cuts the paper. This toy is rare and unusual and should go up in value. Buddy L. toy collectors are not interested in Buddy L accessories now, but we feel they will be in demand in the future.

11 Pot Metal Toys

Kenton Manufacturing Company started business in the 1890s making locks. In 1895 it became Kenton Hardware Manufacturing Company. From the 1920s through the 1950s Kenton manufactured horse-drawn toys, most of which were not marked. This Kenton farm wagon is marked "Made in USA," is 11" long, 4" high, C. 1950, **$45-85.**

Tommy Toys are very similar to Barclay toys, which were also made in the 1930s. These toys are unmarked and there doesn't seem to be a big demand for them. *Left to right:* Doubledecker Bus, C. 1930, 1¼" high, 3" long, **$20-35.** Fire Truck, C. 1930, 1½" high, 4" long, **$30-45.** Gas Tanker, C. 1930, 1½" high, 3½" long, **$25-40.**

Andy Gump's Roadster, made by Tootsie Toy, C. 1930, 1½″ high, 3″ long, **$20-35.**
This looks very much like the Arcade Andy Gump with the same No. 348 on it.
However, the Arcade car is about 7½″ long, 4½″ high, and worth $600-1,000. Value
established by what we paid for the toy.

Fire Truck, made by Hubley, C. 1950, push, 9½″ long, 3″ high, **$32-50.** Driver,
windshield, dash, and ladders are nickel-plated. Value should increase in the future.

12 Push-Pull Toys

Mary Had a Little Lamb, maker unknown, C. 1940, 6″ high, 9½″ long, **$30-45.** Figures are hand-painted papier-mâché, and the wooden wheels are painted.

Girl on Cart, unmarked, litho tin C. 1940, 6¼", 6" high, **$15-25.** Girl twirls as the cart is pulled.

Lithographed tin Rabbit, made in Japan, C. 1930, 5" high, 5" long, **$22-30.** When pulled, back wheels go up and down to make the rabbit "hop."

Dinky Supertoys, England, manufactured many unusual toys. We think they are collectibles of the future. This is a Centurion Tank, C. 1960, 1½" high, 5½" long, **$15-25.**

Cannon of fragile, thin tin, possibly made by Marx, C. 1930, 5" high, 8" long, **$22-30.** Accessory piece for a horse-drawn vehicle.

Toy Tinker, made by Toy Tinkers, Inc., C. 1930, 6¼" high, 8" long, **$27-35.** Wooden toy with metal braces holding the wheels. When pulled, rider bobs up and down.

Flea market special! Touring Car, maker unknown, C. 1930, 3½" high, 8" long, **$20-25.** Wooden body and tin top. Easy to find this toy.

13 Sand-Operated Toys

Sandy Andy — Merry Miller No. 77, made by Wolverine, C. 1920, 12″ high, litho tin, **$80-125.** When the sand comes out of the house and hits the mill wheel, dog chases man back and forth.

Blacksmith, unmarked, C. 1950, 8½″ high, **$20-30.** This is a common sand toy, also made in woodchopper version.

14 Steam Engines and Accessories

Scissor Sharpener, an unusual steam engine accessory, was made in Germany (unmarked), C. 1920, 7" long, 5½" high, **$95-125.** Other accessory pieces are available and worth the same.

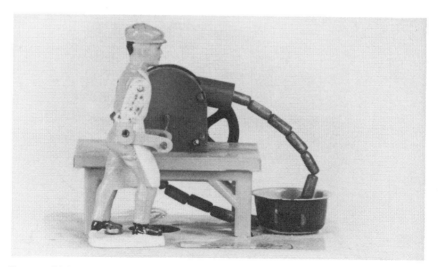

Sausage Maker, by Fleischmann (Germany), C. 1950, 4" high, 5" long, **$65-95.** All tin except hard plastic man. When the man moves arms, sausages go through grinder.

Steam engine, made by Heischmann, 1949, 6½" long, 8" high, worth **$45-65.** The most desirable steam engines are made by Weeden. However, other brands are becoming more popular.

Steam Engine, made by Jensen, C. 1950, electric, 7½" high, 7½" long, **$55-75.** *Not* recommended for children. Builds up steam within three minutes and is very hot and powerful.

15 Streetcars and Trolleys

Trolley Car, unmarked, C. 1930, friction wheel, litho tin, 18½″ long, 6½″ high, **$175-260.** Lever on the front opens the front and back doors. The only mark is a patent number.

Streetcar, made in Japan, C. 1950, friction, 6½" long, 3" high, **$22-38**. Folded lithographed tin with tin wheels. Colorful, nice workmanship. May go up in value.

Cable Car, made in Japan, C. 1940, friction, 7" long, 4½" high, litho tin, **$28-45**. Nicely detailed passengers. Four newer versions of cable cars available, with the most recent being sold in San Francisco gift shops.

16 Tin Toys — Miscellaneous

Northwestern Wagon and Team, made by Northwestern Co., C. 1930, push, 4½″ high, 10¼″ long, **$45-75.** All thin, lithographed tin, except wheels. Very short supply for an American-made toy.

Very fragile Horse-drawn Merry-go-round, maker unknown, C. 1930, push, 10" long, 6" high, **$100-175.** Lithographed horses on merry-go-round are very detailed. Back wheels of the cart activate merry-go-round.

Penny Toy, maker unknown, C. 1930, push, 4½" long, 2¼" high, **$45-65.** Originally sold for a penny in the dime stores during the Depression. Very thin and flimsy.

Pvimal Car, made by Arnold in West Germany, C. 1950, remote control, 3″ high, 9½″ long, **$100-275.** Tin car. Figures in the car are hand-painted papier-mâché. Dashboard detail is hand-painted.

Lazy Day Farms, by Marx, C. 1950, push, 17½″ long, 5½″ high, **$22-30.** Marx made many trucks from 1930-1950. The Coke trucks are the most collectible.

Dump Truck, made by Structo, C. 1950, push, 19" long, 6" high, **$20-35.** Toys made in the 1950s are not in the same demand as those made 1920-1930s.

Coast to Coast Bus Line, made by Wyandotte, C. 1950, push, 20½" long, 6" high, **$45-65.** Unusual bus, with a back door for luggage. Painted metal.

17 Tops

Musical Top with suction cup base, by the M N N Co. (Germany), C. 1940, plunger action, 11½″ high, **$55-75.** When the top spins, plastic figures dance in circles.

Musical Top, by Ohio Art, C. 1960, 6″ long, litho tin, **$7-12.**

18 Trains

Electric

Engine and Coal Car, by American Flyer, C. 1940, 16" long, 5" high, **$100-150.**
Engine is well made in iron and trimmed with brass.

Vintage Locomotive and Coal Car, unmarked, C. 1950, electric, 15" long, 3¼" high,
$100-185. Made of iron trimmed in brass. Motor is mounted in the cab. When the
engine is running in the dark, you can see the look of fire and steam from the engine.

Push-Pull and Ride-on

Train Engine, maker unknown, C. 1920, wheel friction, 4¼" high, 17" long, **$95-125.**
Most 1920s toys were of the heavy wheel friction type and were not popular because of their weight. Also, they didn't work well.

Erie Train Engine, unmarked, C. 1940, ride, 26" long, 10½" high, **$65-100.** Part of a riding train. Not popular because they are dangerous. Painted tin, rough condition.

Train Engine, maker unknown, C. 1930, cast iron, 13½" long, 3¼" high, **$85-125.**
Train is marked "178" and the coal car "P.R.R.," which probably stands for the
Pennsylvania Railroad. Be careful when purchasing this toy, it is being reproduced.
The new model is heavier and thicker cast iron than the original. Also, center axles and
wheels are hollow.

Railway Express car, part of a riding train, painted tin, and in rough condition. It is
unmarked, C. 1940, 23" long, 9½" high, **$55-75.** Note the steering mechanism.

Cor-Cor Pullman, made by Cor-Cor Toys, Washington, Indiana, C. 1940, 24″ long, 9″ high, **$45-75.** Painted tin. Good workmanship.

A very unusual and nicely colored Greatest Show on Earth Circus Train Car, unmarked, 1895, cast iron pull toy, 14½″ long, 6″ high, no established price. Painting on the car looks original. Could be part of a circus train, because this car is marked No. 2.

Cor-Cor Box Car No. 62-26, made by Cor-Cor Toys, Washington, Indiana, C. 1940, 17″ long, 7½″ high, **$45-75.** Painted tin. Good workmanship.

Cor-Cor Caboose No. 62-28, made by Cor-Cor Toys, Washington, Indiana, C. 1940, 17″ long, 8½″ high, **$45-75.** Painted tin. Good workmanship and makes a nice shelf piece.

Pile Driver, made by Hubley, C. 1930, cast iron, 9" long, 12" high, **$125-195.** When cranked to the top, it releases the pile driver. It's difficult to find this toy with the original pile driver in it.

Windup

Overland Flyer, unmarked, tin, C. 1930, 29½″ long, **$70-110.** Front of engine and the back pullman car are lighted by batteries.

Engine and Cars, maker unknown, C. 1930, 23″ long, **$85-150.** This is mostly tin with some cast iron. The coal car is marked "B & O Railroad" and the passenger cars are marked "Niagara."

This train could possibly be a penny toy. Made in the 1930s, maker unknown, 9″ long, 2″ high, **$30-40.** Made of very thin tin. The engine is marked "Rico," and the passenger car is marked "Renfe." Could be hand-painted.

19 Windup Toys

Animals

Flipping Dog, made in Japan, C. 1950, litho tin, 4½″ long, **$22-30.** Colorful with a lot of action. Hard to find with original cloth shoe in mouth. Company made dogs, cats, cars, airplanes, and horses that rolled over. Airplanes, horses, and cars are worth more money.

Left to right: One-Rabbit Band, made in Japan, 1950s, 6½" high, **$25-32.** Plays drum and cymbal. Cocktail Shaker, made in Japan, C. 1950s, 7" high, **$25-32.** A one action toy.

Three Fuzzy Animals, made in Japan, C. 1950, 2½" high, **$12-20 each.** These animals didn't last long as the fuzz fell off with use. If found in the original box, can each be worth $5-10 more.

Left to right: Carrot-Eating Rabbit, made in Japan, C. 1950, 4½" high, **$22-25.** One action toy. Animal Swing, made in Japan, C. 1950, 7" high, **$22-25.** One action toy.

Hen and chicks, made in Japan, C. 1960, 3" high, **$8-12.** Cute plastic toy. Hen pecks "corn."

Hopping Rabbit, made in Japan, C. 1950, 5" high, **$9-15.** This toy has tin ears and feet with no cottontail. Others had plastic ears and feet and cottontails.

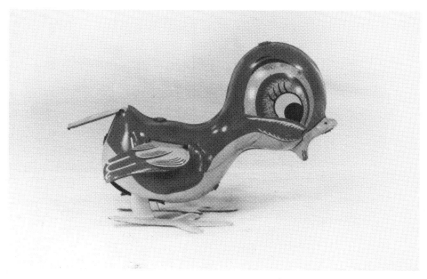

Hopping Bird, made by Mikuni of Japan, C. 1960, litho tin, 4" long, 3½" high, **$12-20.** When this toy jumps, its tail and wings flap. Made in China today and marked "Made in China."

Jumping Horse, made by Daiya, Japan, C. 1960, 4½" long, 5½" high, **$17-25.** This toy is exactly like a toy made in China today. The Chinese toy is worth $7.50.

Squirrel, made in Japan, C. 1950, litho tin, 2½" high, 3½" long, **$10-15.** Moves across surface, but will not move in straight line.

Jumping Horse, made in Japan, C. 1950, litho tin, 4½″ long, **$32-45.** Made with either a rubber Indian or cowboy rider.

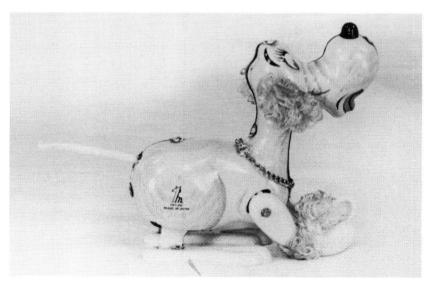

Jumping Dog, Mikun, Japan, C. 1960, 5″ long, **$10-17.** Tin with plastic legs. Ears and leg trim are fake fur.

Dachshund, made in Japan, C. 1950, windup, 5½″ long, **$25-35.** Moves quickly across surface.

Clever Bear, made in Japan (marked with paper seal), 1948, 5½″ long, **$35-50.** Lots of action. Bear walks, stops, moves head back and forth, growls, and repeats.

Begging Scottie, made by Y of Japan, C. 1950, windup, 6¼″ high, **$25-30.** Dog scoots across surface, tail spins, and he barks. Should increase in value.

Flossing Rabbit, made in Japan, C. 1950, 6″ high, **$22-28.** Similar to the Knitting Kitty in action. This rabbit is missing its one, long, front tooth.

Drummer Bear, made in Japan, C. 1950, 6″ high, **$25-35.** Bear moves
head and drums.

Bear Cleaning Glasses, Japan, C. 1950, 7″ high, **$32-42.** Bear moves his feet, removes glasses, wipes glasses, and returns them to place.

Farmer's Milk, made in Japan, C. 1950, 6" high, **$25-35.** This toy is very much like a later battery toy made in the 1960s.

Reading Bear, made in Japan, C. 1950, windup, 5″ high, **$22-36.** The bear's head moves up and down as he flips the pages of book.

Knitting Granny, made in Japan, C. 1950, 6″ high, **$32-42.** The kitty knits. Most of the Japanese toys made in the 1950s were fuzzy animals.

Horse Race Derby, made in Japan, C. 1950, 6½″ long, **$32-42.** Base circles as the horses rock up and down.

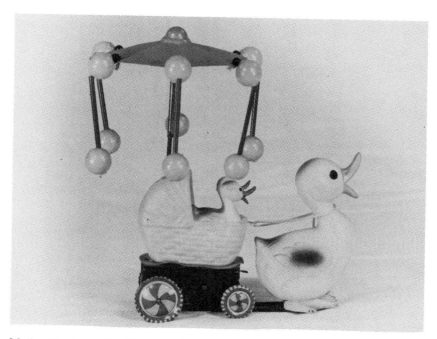

Mother Duck and Ducklings, made in Japan, C. 1940, 6″ high, 5″ long, **$40-55.** Celluloid except for the tin base and wheels. Very fragile. We think the value could be higher.

By Chein

Barnacle Bill, C. 1940, 6″ high, **$100-160.** Good lithographed tin. Looks a lot like Popeye.

Roller Coaster, C. 1950, litho tin, 19″ long, 10½″ high, **$60-95.** Always came with two cars that rode the track. Chein made another roller coaster in 1938 that depicted a sideshow. The value is about the same. The picture on this toy is a hot dog stand.

Native Riding Turtle, C. 1950, litho tin, 4½″ high, 8″ long, **$65-100.** Cute, but highly overrated.

Very fragile Yellow Taxi, Main 7570, C. 1930, windup, 6" long, 3" high, **$50-95.** Made from very thin litho tin.

From England

English Sedan, C. 1930, tin, 11" long, 4" high, **$145-225.** "Dunlop 90" on tires. Should increase in value.

Germany and U. S. Zone Germany

Crazy Cat, made in Germany, C. 1920, 6″ high, **$100-225.** Similar to Felix the Cat made in the late 1920s. Felix is marked and has a flatter, more rounded nose. This toy is unmarked.

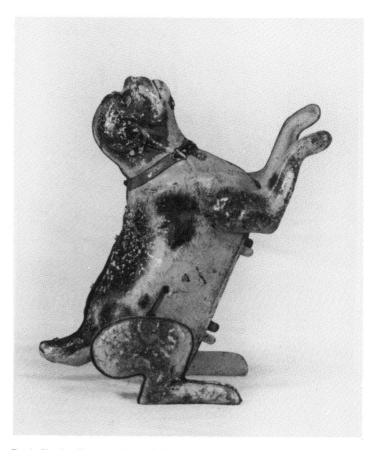

Back-flipping Dog, made by S.G. Germany, C. 1930, litho tin, 5½″ high, **$40-65.** Made in black and white, brown and white, and red and white. Does back-flips when wound.

Gunfighter, made in U.S. Zone Germany, C. 1940, litho tin, 9″ high, **$35-48.** When wound, upper body moves back and forth while eyes move in opposite direction.

Jolly Monkey, made in West Germany, C. 1950, 7″ high, **$30-40.**
Excellent quality, similar to Steiff. Note paper tag in ear.

Another monkey with a tagged ear, made in West Germany, C. 1950, 7¼" high, **$38-45.** There were four of these animals made with this particular tag. The others are: Rabbit Shaking Rattles; Monkey Drumming; and Bear Playing a Cymbal.

Ferris Wheel, made in Germany, C. 1890, 17" high, **$600-950**. Toy was made from iron and tin, hand-painted, has clockwork mechanism, and is chain-driven. Only men are found sitting in the ferris wheel seats because it was not considered ladylike for women to ride the ferris wheel in the Gay Nineties.

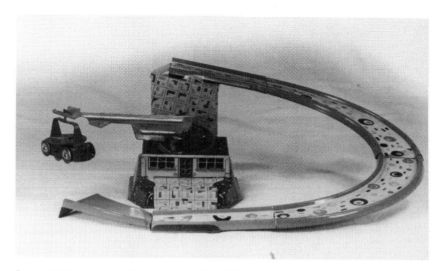

Carnival Ride, made in Germany, C. 1950, 4″ high, 8″ long, **$32-45.** Great action toy. The arm over the building picks up the car, carries it to the top of the toy, releases it, and the car comes down the curved track with its bell ringing.

Cat and Mouse, made in Germany, C. 1920, windup, 8½″ long, **$65-95.** Friction plates inside the head of cat make eyes light up and spark as the cat chases mouse.

145

Train engine with very unusual winding mechanism and front wheel drive. Very thin litho tin. Made by Orobr of Germany, C. 1920, windup, 6″ long, 3½″ high, **$55-95.**

Replica 1913 Mercer, made by Schuco, West Germany, C. 1950, 2½″ high, 6½″ long, **$60-95.** Very beautiful, lithographed tin, excellent quality and detail. Has two shift levers. One for forward and reverse; the other to start and stop.

Horse-drawn Sulky, made in Germany, C. 1950, 6½″ long, **$45-65.** The horse and driver are plaster cast and hand-painted. Very fragile. Legs move mechanically.

Horse and Cart, marked G&K-509, Germany, C. 1930, 4½″ high, 7″ long, **$295-325.** Very distinct lithograph on tin. Toy rocks back and forth similar to later versions of Marx toys. Very fragile and delicate.

MG, made in Germany, C. 1940, windup, 9½″ long, 2½″ high, **$95-125.** Marked U.S. Zone Germany on the bottom and has a working steering wheel, shift lever, first, second, and third gears, reverse, and an on and off switch. Also came in yellow, red, and gray, and made in Jaguar styling.

Pool Players, made in Germany but unmarked, C. 1920, litho tin, 15″ long, **$95-145.** Toy was sold in a box with chips and black and white marbles. The table and box are marked with numbers to record points as the players shoot pool. Very rare to find the box and parts, and worth an additional $50.

Motorcycle and Rider, made by Arnold, U.S. Zone Germany, C. 1940, litho tin, 7½″ long, **$25-45.** Very good detail.

Japanese Character

Circus Clown (short and tall) made in Japan, C. 1950, 8″-9½″ high, **$50-65.** Made like the Schuco Charlie Chaplin in the 1920s.

Hillbilly Band, made by Alps, Japan, C. 1950, 4″ plus **$50-75** for set of three. Hard plastic figures have tin feet and wear cloth hats. They dance in circles while their necks stretch up and down.

Baby Walker, made in Japan, C. 1960, 4¼″ high, **$32-48.** Add $5-10 if found in original box.

Crazy Waiter, made by Yone, Japan, C. 1960, litho tin, 6½″ high, **$15-25.** Waiter walks along a surface ringing bell.

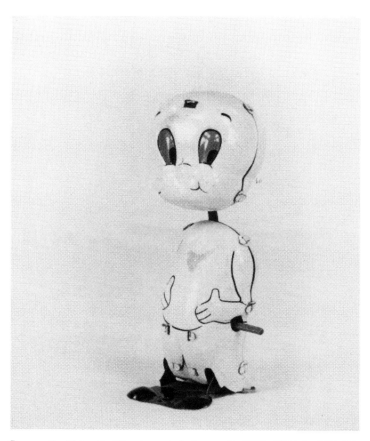

Casper the Friendly Ghost, made in Japan, C. 1960, 5″ high, **$12-22.**
One action jumping toy.

Dancing Man, made in Japan, C. 1930, base windup, litho tin, 7½" high, **$85-125.** Very hard to find in the original box.

Drummer Boy, made in Japan, C. 1940, 6″ high, **$30-40.** Revolutionary War figure, hard to find in good working condition.

Santa Claus and Reindeer, C. 1930, w/celluloid, 6" high, **$45-65.** Toy is completely made of celluloid, and could have been made in Occupied Japan. Lots of action.

Moon Mars Ride, made by T. C., Japan, C. 1960, 12½″ high, **$50-65.**
Good litho tin with action. The airplanes spin around, the men in the
tower move in the opposite direction, and a bell rings.

Season's Greetings, C. 1960, 6″ long, **$8-12**. This is an inexpensive toy unless you find the original box, in which case, the toy is worth an additional $25. The box says, "Greetings from the North Pole." Helicopter is Santa Claus.

Japanese Rarities

Circus Horse Ring, made by Tokyo Shei, C. 1930, 5½″ high, **$75-125** (MIB). Some of these toys were made with acrobat on the horse. Action: clown raises the flag and baton up and down while rocking back and forth. Horse circles. The acrobat on the horse twirled.

Left to right: Scooting Baby, C. 1940, celluloid, 6", **$30-42.** It scoots along a surface, stops, and scoots again. We have seen celluloid dolls with no action sell for more money and feel that this toy is undervalued at the moment. Celluloid Bear Clown, C. 1930, 8" high, **$30-45.** The bear moves along a surface, does somersault. Very unique and unusual for an early Japanese toy.

By Lehmann

Lehmann toys were made in Germany and are difficult to find in excellent condition and working order. They are very clearly marked.

Alabama Coon Jigger, 1914, litho tin, 10″ high, **$295-425.** There are two versions of this toy. The more expensive one, pictured, has the trip lever on the side. The other version has the trip lever on the front.

Anxious Bride, 1910, 8½″ long, **$700-1,200.** Impossible to find this toy with the original paper hanky in the bride's hand.

Red Cycle, 1927, 5″ long, **$100-185.** Not to be confused with the front end of the Anxious Bride toy.

Drum Major, maker unknown, but frequently mistaken for a Lehmann. C. 1890, 8½″ high, **$70-95.** Very hard to find in good condition. Not much of a market for this toy and not a good investment unless found in mint condition.

Lithographed tin beetle, C. 1890, 2¼″ high, 3½″ long, **$55-95.** One of the early Lehmann toys. Runs along a surface and flaps its wings. Not a very desirable toy even at its age.

Masuyama, 1913, 6½" long, **$525-975.** Most of the time the original umbrella or fan will be missing with reproductions substituted.

Ampol, C. 1903-1907, 5" high, 5" long, **$780-1,200.** Very rare to find this toy with the original steering stick and the globe umbrella.

By Lindstrom

Mammy, C. 1930, 8″ high, **$70-125.** Very seldom found in original box.
Mammy shakes as she walks.

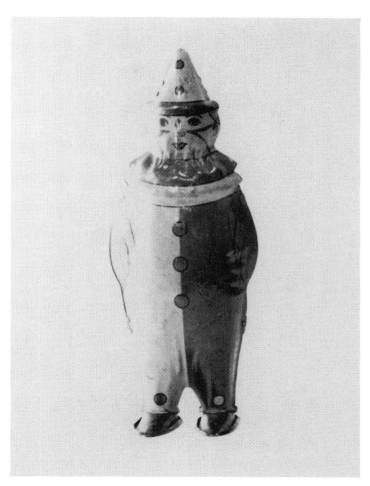

Johnny, C. 1930, 8¼" high, **$90-125.** Lindstrom made five shaking walkers. This clown is the hardest to find.

Betty, C. 1930, 8″, **$70-125.** Seldom found in original box.

Marx Comic Characters

Milton Berle Car, 1953, 5½" long, 6" high, litho tin, **$95-135.** Writing on all four sides of car. Milton wears a plastic hat. Seldom find the hat unbroken.

Charlie McCarthy, 1935, litho tin, 8" long, 6" high, **$160-250.** The car moves back and forth as Charlie's head makes a complete circle.

Harold Lloyd, C. 1930, 11″ high, litho tin, **$175-300.** Body moves and face moves in and out of a smile.

Mortimer Snerd, C. 1930, litho tin, 8½″ high, **$95-150.** He waddle-walks, tips his hat, has very good detail and color.

Amos 'N' Andy Fresh Air Taxi, C. 1930, litho tin, 8″ long, 5″ high, **$300-500.** Car moves, stops, shakes, and then repeats the action.

Popeye carrying parrots in cages, C. 1930, litho tin, 8″ high, **$120-220.**
Value of toy depends on whether original pipe and/or box are found. Most
were marked on the left side "Louis Marx." Ten percent were not
marked. This toy is not marked and slightly larger than the marked
version.

Joe Penner Wanna Buy a Duck, C. 1930, 8″ high, litho tin, **$145-245.**
Joe walks, his hat tips, and the cigar moves up and down.

Others by Marx

Left to right: Drumming native, 1957, 6½" high, **$35-50.** This toy made in Japan and assembled by the Louis Marx Co. in the U.S. Rabbit on Tricycle was made by Suzunk, Japan, C. 1950, 4" long, 4½" high, **$18-25.** Rabbit is celluloid; tricycle is litho tin. Hard to find in working condition.

George, the Drummer Boy, C. 1930, litho tin, 9″ high, **$65-95.** Marx made two drummer boys, one with movable eyes, and one with stationary eyes. Same size and value.

Acrobatic Marvel, C. 1930, very nice litho tin, 13½″ high, 7½″ long, **$75-95.** Notice circus characters on base. The base rocks as monkey does acrobatic tricks. Monkey has hard paper, jointed legs.

Range Rider rocking platform, C. 1950, 11" long, 10" high. **$60-100.** Marx also made the Lone Ranger, Ride 'Em Cowboy, Hopalong Cassidy, etc. All have about the same value except 1950 television cowboys. They are higher in value. Add $20 for an original box.

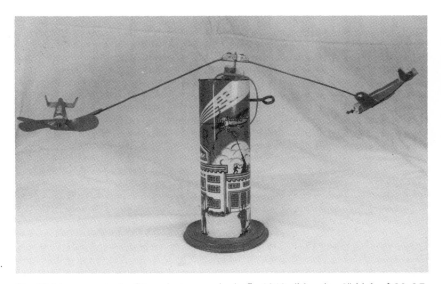

Sky Fighters, made by Marx but unmarked, C. 1940, litho tin, 8" high, **$60-95.** Planes fly around the tower and their propellers go around. Marx also made the Sky Bird Flyer and Sky Rangers. All have about the same value.

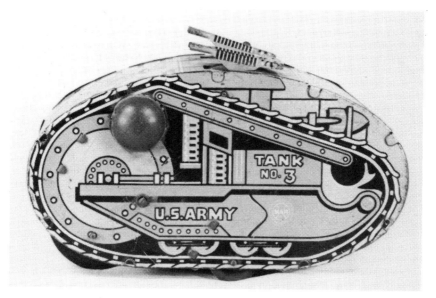

U.S. Army Tank No. 3, C. 1940, litho tin, 8″ long, 4½″ high, **$45-75.** Very noisy as it moves and the two guns spark. Marx made many war toys in the 1940s.

Turnover Tank No. 5, C. 1940, litho tin, 4″ long, 3″ high, **$22-35.** Has wooden wheels, moves along a surface and flips over.

Ring-a-Ling Circus, C. 1930, litho tin, 8½" high, base 8", **$145-290.** This is early version. Later version is smaller with less detail on the animals and ringmaster. Both have equal value. We have never seen either in their original boxes. The ringmaster goes around and touches each animal with his baton. As he does this, the clown spins, elephant rears up, monkey climbs the pole, and the lion rears up.

New York Circular with Train, C. 1920, litho tin, base 8", **$120-195.** Marx made the Honeymoon Express, Subway Express, and Mickey Mouse train in the same way with the windup mechanism in the middle. Some had airplanes on top that flew around. All have about the same value.

Sandy, Little Orphan Annie's Dog, C. 1940, 5" long, 4¼" high, **$110-185.** Sandy is more expensive with the suitcase in his mouth. If Sandy keeps falling down, this means that the wiring in his legs is loose. This is very difficult to fix.

Peter Rabbit Eccentric Car, C. 1950, 8" high, 6" long, **$45-75.** Wheels are litho tin, rest is plastic. The rabbit's head goes around in circles and his ears flip back and forth.

Race Car 711, C. 1940, 12½" long, **$25-50.** Marx made race cars from 5" to 27" long. Easy to find and very collectible.

Whoopee Car, C. 1930, litho tin, 8" long, 6" high, **$60-100.** Has laughing cows on the wheels. Another similar car had peanuts on the wheels. The one with the peanuts is worth about $50 more than this one.

Queen of the Campus, C. 1940, 5½" long, 5½" high, **$95-125.** This toy is litho tin with a plastic boy. It is similar to Joy Ride made in 1929 with a college boy driving the car. Action is the same. Car moves back and forth and the boy's head moves.

Joy Rider, C. 1928-1929, litho tin, 7" long, 6" high, **$145-195.** The Joy Rider moves back and forth while head turns in circles. Note the print on the car. Rarely find this toy with the suitcase on back of car.

Sam the Gardener, C. 1950, 7½" high, 8" long, **$45-65.** Cart is litho tin; plastic man wears cloth outfit. When wound, the man walks behind the cart.

Balky Mule, C. 1930, litho tin, 8½" long, **$50-75.** The driver bounces as the cart moves back and forth. Marx mark is located under the mule.

Royal Van Co., 1929-1933, 4½" high, 9" long, **$60-85.** Made from very thin, folded tin with nice lithography. Hard to find with original driver.

Police Motorcycle and Sidecar, C. 1940, 8" long, 5½" high, **$90-145.** This tin toy is elaborately lithographed. It has a siren and the front sparks.

Mystic Motorcycle, C. 1930, litho tin, 3″ high, 4½″ long, **$50-75.** When the motorcycle comes to the end of a surface, it will not fall off, but will turn around and continue on its way. We feel that the value of this toy has peaked at this point.

P.D. Motorcycle, 1935, litho tin, 5½″ high, 8¼″ long, **$65-110.** When it runs, the siren howls.

Miscellaneous Makers

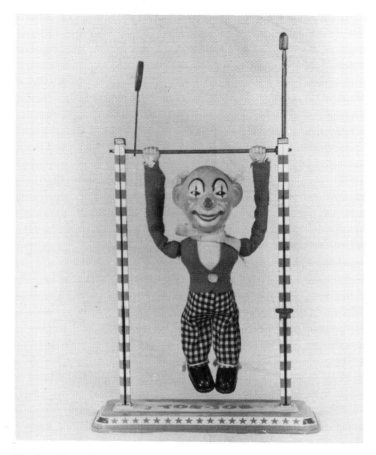

Toe-Joe Circus Acrobat, made by Ohio Art, C. 1950, lever action, 12″ high, **$30-45.**

Charlie Chapman, unmarked, C. 1930, 8½" high, litho tin, **$375-695.**
Chaplin's body rocks back and forth, and has cast iron shoes. Price
quoted is with original arms and cane and is very difficult to find.

1904 Round Dash Oldsmobile, made by Hefner, C. 1930, 10½" long, 6"
high, **$1,000-1,400.** Windup crank is mounted on the back with a four
position steering arm in front. Original color was drab green. Has a
wooden seat with material cover. Probably not a good investment at this
price.

Drummer Boy, made by Wolverine, C. 1930-1940, litho tin, 14"
high, **$65-85.** The drummer rocks back and forth as he plays the
drum. The 7" size is cheaper.

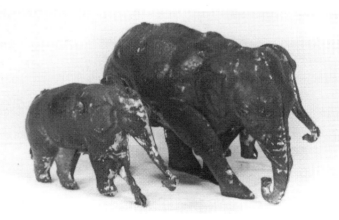

Walking Elephants, maker unknown, C. 1920, 4½" long, 3¼" high, **$125-195.**
Fragile tin. The babies walking move the mother.

Tom Twist, or The Funny Clown, made by Strauss, C. 1930, 8½"
high, **$75-125.** Toy is missing some parts (bells on ears and arms),
but complete is worth a great deal more. When the toy works, the
clown stands on his head and his legs rock back and forth.

Jocko the Golfer, made in the U.S.A., C. 1930, string operated, 6½″ long, 6½″ high, **$125-225.** Pull the string and the golfer hits the ball. Make sure the string is whole — it is almost impossible to fix.

Cowboy on Jumping Horse, unmarked, C. 1910 +, litho tin, 6″ high, 6½″ long, **$225-300.** Similar to the George Washington on Horseback toy. George Washington horse is white and toy was marked. Both have same value, but collectors prefer the George Washington model.

Kid-Samson, made by Selrite U.S.A. (B & R mark), 1927, litho tin, 8½"
high, **$225-400.** When Kid-Samson lifts his hammer and hits the lever, a
metal ball runs up to the top and rings a bell.

Left to right: Whistling Boy, unmarked, C. 1940, plastic, 9½" high, **$32-45.** When wound, the boy shuffles about and whistles. Goose, made by Playtime, C. 1960, push down, 4" high, **$8-12.** Cheap giveaway toy. Push goose down and she lays an egg. Not much demand at this time. Pecos Pete, made by Marx, C. 1960, 8½" high, **$12-20.** Future collectible. Hard to find not broken. Will become more desirable as older Marx toys disappear.

By Unique Art Co.

G. I. Joe and his Bouncing Jeep, C. 1940, litho tin, 6½" high, 6¼" long, **$65-125.** An easy toy for the beginning collector to find, but about 50 percent do not work.

Freight Wagon, C. 1940, litho tin, 15" long, 6¼" high, **$55-85.** Back wheels are tin, front wheels are rubber traction. We have seen this toy with plastic suitcases and sacks on the back. However, it was originally empty, as far as we know.

G. I. Joe and the K-9 Pups, C. 1940, litho tin, 9″ high, **$65-95.** Walks along a surface.

Li'l Abner and his Dogpatch Band, 1945, 10″ long, 8″ high, **$250-395.** Lithographed tin with great action. Li'l Abner dances, Mammy directs, Pappy plays the drum, and Daisy Mae plays the piano. Hard to find with all the characters in place and working. Make sure Mammy has her pipe.

Left to right: Roll-Over Plane and Scooter Clown, both made in China, C. 1980, windup, 3″-5″, **$6-12.** Both are copies of toys made in the 1950s.

Duck and Dog Cart, made in China, C. 1980, windup, 5½″ long, **$20.** Toy is celluloid and hard plastic and is a four action toy. It moves along a surface, the umbrella spins, duck bobs head up and down, and the dog jumps up and down.

Jumping Burro, made in China, C. 1980, windup, 5″ long, **$7-12.**

Donkey and Clown Cart, made in the U.S.S.R., C. 1980, windup, 7½″ long, **$22.** This is a new version of a 1940s Marx toy.

Shutter Bug, made in China, C. 1980, windup and battery, 5″ high, **$7-12.** This toy looks like the original Shutter Bug made by T. N. Co. in the 1950s. Toy moves, stops, lifts camera, flashes light on camera.

Left to right: Frog, Bird, Rabbit, and Duck, all made in China, C. 1980, windup, 2″-3″, **$2 each.** Collectibles of the future.

Carnival Ride, made in West Germany, C. 1970, windup, 6½" high, **$22-25.**

Ladybugs, made in China, C. 1980, windup, 10" long, **$4.** Copy of the original made in the 1950s by Chein.

Porter Boy is a copy of a toy made in the 1940s. Original had a tin head and body. This toy has a rubber head and body and was made in China, C. 1980, windup, 4½″ high, **$12.**

Left to right: Drumming Bear, Girl Riding Swan, Parcel Post Delivery, all made in China, C. 1980, windup, 3½″ high, **$7-12.** Girl Riding Swan is made of celluloid. Cute with lots of action.

Left to right: Elephant Riding Scooter, marked U. S. Zone, Germany, C. 1980, windup, 6½″ high. It is new version of 1940s U.S. Zone Germany toy. This toy has thin plastic wheels, while the original had hard rubber wheels. **$22.** Duck Riding Scooter, marked U. S. Zone Germany, C. 1980, windup, 6½″ high. New version of 1940s U.S. Zone Germany toy. This toy has thin plastic wheels. Original had hard rubber wheels. **$22.**

Elf Ride, made in West Germany, C. 1970, windup, 5½″ high, **$22-25.**

Bibliography

Periodicals
Antique Toy World, 3941 Belle Plaine, Chicago, Illinois.

Books
Cranmer, Don. *Collectors Encyclopedia Toys, Banks with Prices.* Marion, Indiana: L-W Books, 1983.

O'Brien, Richard. *Collecting Toys: A Collector's Identification and Value Guide.* Florence, Alabama: Books Americana, Inc. 1985.

Schorr, Martyn L. *Guide to Mechanical Toy Collecting.* Haworth, N. J.: Performance Media, 1979.

About the Authors

Yesterday's Toys with Today's Prices is Fred and Marilyn Fintel's first book on antique and collectible toys. Fred has been collecting and repairing toys and toy-related items for more than twenty-five years. In the past five years he has shown his toys at antique shows from Arizona to Wisconsin and has also appeared on television shows in Arizona and Texas lecturing and demonstrating his toys. Fred has written newspaper articles and also given lectures at local clubs. His knowledge and expertise is widely recognized in the toy collecting field. All of the toys photographed in this book are from Fred's personal collection.

Marilyn Fintel and daughter Desiree share Fred's love and interest in this fascinating hobby. The family has traveled from coast to coast attending antique auctions and buying toys, dolls, and glassware to add to their collections.